Written by Demola Allen
13th & Joan Publishing House

ADINO'S WORLD. Copyright 2024 by Demola Allen.

All rights reserved. No part of this publication may be reproduced, distributed, or transmitted in any form or by any means, including photocopying, recording, or other electronic or mechanical methods, without the prior written permission of the publisher, except in the case of brief quotations embodied in critical reviews and certain other noncommercial uses permitted by copyright law.

For permission requests, write to the publisher, addressed "Attention: Permissions Coordinator," 205 N. Michigan Avenue, Suite #810, Chicago, IL 60601. 13th & Joan books may be purchased for educational, business or sales promotional use.

For information, please email the Sales Department at sales@13thandjoan.com. Printed in the U. S. A.

First Printing, January 2024

Library of Congress Cataloging-in-Publication Data has been applied for.

ISBN: 978-1-7322479-0-1

I dedicate this book to the memory of my mother, Fayetta Allen, and my cousin, Dionne Arceneaux.

Epigraph

Your world is a reflection of your mind.

INTRODUCTION

It's after school and Adino is in his room playing with his toys. He notices that many of his toys have cool jobs. He has toys that work as ninjas, firefighters, superheros, and race car drivers and he can't help but to think,

"I want a cool job when I grow up. So what will it be?"

"My Mom is a teacher and my Dad works in a lab but what do I want to do with my life?"

He realizes the question he just asked himself is a serious one and he needs to figure it out.

One Hour later

24 hours later

1440 minutes later

86400 seconds later

"Recess will last 30 minutes longer!!"

"That's my young man!"

"And students will go on field trips once a week!"

"Ooo I wanna come to your school!"

"Sorry, you're too old. Security!!!"

"Moooom!"

36

later that day

Hello!

Now it's your turn to make a great sandwich.
I left you an, easy and fun recipe for
you to follow with the option to add your
favorite jelly.

My favorite is strawberry.
Make sure to ask for your parents' permission
before you start.

Recipe for Adino's famous chicken nugget, honey, potato chip, waffle and cheese, 3 pickles, jelly sandwich.

Ingredients for one:

- 2 waffles
- 3-5 chicken nuggets
- jelly of choice
- honey
- 1 tsp butter
- chips of choice
- slice of cheese
- 3 pickles

Serving and directions:

Heat the chicken nuggets separately. Butter both sides of the waffles, then spread honey on the waffles. Take a slice of cheese and cut it in half. Place one half of the cheese on both sides of the waffles, then place the chicken nuggets on one waffle. Add jelly on top of the chicken nuggets, then add chips, and 3 pickles.

Put the other waffle on top to make a sandwich, and flatten using a spatula. Place the sandwich in the oven at 350* temperature until the cheese is melted. Once the cheese is melted, take it out of the oven and enjoy! Parental supervision recommended.

About The Author

Demola works as a lab scientist and an author in Houston, Tx. He lives with his wife and two children.

Connect With Demola

Instagram: @DemolAdino
Facebook: Demola Allen

www.ingramcontent.com/pod-product-compliance
Lightning Source LLC
Chambersburg PA
CBHW042355070526
44585CB00028B/2934